GREAT INTERACTIONS

Luke and Mikey, Endeavour Academy, Oxfordshire

GREAT INTERACTIONS

Life with Learning
Disabilities and Autism

A photo-essay
by Polly Braden

In partnership
with MacIntyre

Dewi Lewis Publishing

Charles used his climbing sessions to complete the physical element of his Bronze Duke of Edinburgh Award. This was a huge achievement for him. Charles enjoys the cooperative work he does whilst climbing, traversing from side to side. We use bean bags and hoops to play games and make the wall more engaging and challenging. Charles's climbing sessions have a huge benefit on his overall health and wellbeing: the exercise he receives, the sensory feedback he gets from holding his own body weight and the feel of the rough surface of the holds, as well as the social interaction from staff and his peers, are all invaluable.

Callum, behaviour support specialist, MacIntyre School Wingrave, Buckinghamshire

—

I have been working with Charles for a year. We use PECS (Picture Exchange Communication System) to help him form sentences instead of using single words. With the visual prompt from his PECS he now says, 'I want apple please Joanna' instead of just 'apple'. This helps him to build his vocabulary.

He eats a lot, but is quite thin. I think it is because of his anxiety. He forms strong attachments to men particularly. He witnessed his father's death. He died of a heart attack. Charles is very bright; he understands more than people give him credit for. When it is a very anxious time for him he can fall back to old habits and it can take some time for him to recover. We realised this is often around his father's birthday or another trigger connected to him. He starts to run off frequently, or he laughs nervously (this is very different from his usual joyous laugh). We have started to make him a 'life stories' book. It is a photo book of life before coming to MacIntyre School and of his time since moving here. It helps him to calm down. We can talk through things using this visual prompt which reassures him.

Joanna, class teacher, MacIntyre School Wingrave, Buckinghamshire

Rebecca joined MacIntyre School Wingrave in 2011 when she was just 13 years old. Within a month she turned 14 and had her first MacIntyre birthday party. We filled the house with her favourite things, played her favourite music and invited lots of people. Rebecca at this point was still very new to us, and us to her. We quickly realised this was not her ideal birthday and we had some learning to do. Rebecca really struggled with the transition to new environments even if it was something she enjoyed, working with unfamiliar staff members, sharing the computer, eating at the table with others. In her time at Wingrave we have watched Rebecca go from a shy and anxious young girl into a wonderfully confident and elegant young lady. She loves *Who wants to be a millionaire?,* intensive interaction, dancing and her own reflection! Rebecca has a core group of dance moves that she has perfected over the years and ensures the staff copying her have got them right too. Building relationships with new people has been Rebecca's biggest challenge and the one we have been keenest to help her get right. By using skills such as warmth, being responsive and using Rebecca's preferred method of communication, we quickly started to overcome these obstacles to start pushing some serious boundaries! Rebecca has just spent her 17th birthday with us. Seeing the very obvious improvements she has made makes my job very special.

Vickie, My Way facilitator, MacIntyre School Wingrave, Buckinghamshire

Rebecca with Lisa, MacIntyre School Wingrave, Buckinghamshire

Gemma is autistic. I sat down to talk with her at a sports hall in Milton Keynes with a support worker, Sara Smith. Gemma averts her gaze but tries her best to answer my questions about what she does at day care services. She likes drawing butterflies and gardening but doesn't like sport as it makes her feel sick. Her mind moves in quick jumps. Next she wants to talk about *EastEnders*.

Gemma finds it hard to express herself. Sara and her team try to keep Gemma on an even keel. If she begins to feel irritated by someone or something it can often snowball into great anger. So a major task of the support team is to understand what it is that Gemma needs to convey.

Polly

The centre offers a broad curriculum to learners in a wide range of vocational, work-based and community settings.

I remember one time arriving at MacIntyre Abingdon Partnership (MAP) College, where there is an educational programme, called No Limits, which is tailored to each student. Mikey was at the top of a stairwell with two members of staff trying to coax him down. Later that same day, I saw him running towards a gap in the hedge. Luckily two support workers managed to catch up with him just before he reached the busy road. Last year he was found a place at Endeavour Academy, a newly opened school for autistic children, which is better suited to Mikey's needs and a safer environment for him.

I catch up with Scott for a chat: 'Working with Mikey last year was such a joy. He was a combination of Tigger from *Winnie the Pooh* and the Road Runner! You definitely needed a lot of energy when working with him. Mikey loves to play ball games, particularly football. He is very talented, often kicking the ball over the college fence! Mikey made a big impact and has left great memories for the team who supported him in his year at No Limits.'

Polly talks to Scott, community learning facilitator, MAP College

Mikey (right) with Scott, MAP College

Mikey moved to Endeavour Academy, a newly opened school for autistic children aged 11–21, last year. He is one of the funniest guys. Sadly I am not in his classroom any more, but I see him every day, and I do some overtime on Wednesdays at After School Club mainly because this is the day Mikey attends, so I can still spend some quality time with him. He says something like 'Hello, Raulie Waulie', and we play in the garden, or play the stolen-nose game or whatever else he likes to do.

Mikey is an extremely social person, as if he wanted to burst the myth of the isolated and aloof autistic person. He can say the most shocking and fun things and has great timing with a verbal joke. Someone might have been complaining about something and the next minute Mikey goes over smiling, pats him on the shoulder and says, with his cracked voice, 'Shh, it's alright, you are a good boy'. And you can't help but laugh.

Mikey has problems, of course. He can't make sense of much of the world around him. He struggles especially with transitions: he can't move from one activity to the next, which causes him a great deal of anxiety. He also has no sense of danger whatsoever, so he needs to be supported just to go out shopping. On a bad day Mikey will just sit somewhere and ask to go home. He will refuse to engage in any activity or even come to the classroom. He can be physically challenging as well, although this is very rare. Getting Mikey involved in any educational activity is hard work, and we are very happy when he joins for just a few minutes. He needs this kind of support: he needs to be around people who know and understand him, who are willing to go a step further and discover the bright and amazing person he is.

Raúl, higher-level teaching assistant, Endeavour Academy, Oxfordshire

Adam is 18 and lives with his family in Abingdon. He attends MacIntyre Abingdon Partnership (MAP) College which provides specialist day placements for people aged 16–25 with complex learning disablilties and autism.

I've known Adam for almost two years. When we first met it was very difficult to do any activity with him: he barely used one or two words. He has made great progress and he can now stay sitting at a table with other children for a while. Because he likes putting things in their right place, he would take someone's pencil if he wanted to tidy up. But slowly, he has learned that this is not the best way to behave. Now, he is more able to share space with others.

One of the keys to helping autistic children to make sense of the world is maintaining a routine. Having the same people using the same consistent techniques every day makes the world a little more understandable and easier to cope with. Adam likes to go shopping, and creates routines for that too. To begin with he learned to take a bag of crisps and go straight to the till, but I could not help him to pick up additional items for his dinner, for example. We succeeded finally, and now Adam can shop properly. It took a lot of work though! Without help he would just stay at home, with only a glimpse of the outside world.

Adam needs to develop strategies to live in society and have access to a meaningful life, and even to enjoy himself. When he feels safe he is great to be around and occasionally he even has an explosion of joy. One time, in a music session, he was really enjoying himself listening to *Smells Like Teen Spirit* by Nirvana, and started using my back as drums. It was one of these few beautiful moments in which, for whatever reason, the whole class was taking part and having fun with it. They loved the song so much that we played it three times. And Adam turned and hugged me! Memories like these are precious and I feel the need to treasure them.

Raúl, higher-level teaching assistant, MAP College, Oxfordshire

Following spread: Aja lives in Banbury with her mother and siblings. She is supported by MacIntyre No Limits. Her support has been designed, by her support worker and family, specifically to prepare Aja for the future. She has two-to-one support and is learning social skills such as how to eat in public and how to get about on public transport. Polly

Adam (left) with Raúl, MAP College, Oxfordshire

Aja with Farah, MacIntyre No Limits, Oxfordshire

New Routes: Horticulture and Woodwork Project was set up fifteen years ago, as a therapeutic centre for people with learning disabilities and autism. We started with five learners coming between one and three times a week. Now thirty learners come every week. We sell produce to people who come to the park and we have just been to our first farmers' market.

I learn a lot from the people who come. There's so much to do, but the emphasis is always on people enjoying themselves. We have to keep them going. Having an end product is fantastic; being able to see things grow, the cycle of work through the seasons and enjoying the harvest are great motivators. Plants make you slow down and in fact learners here show you that too. Each time they come you see them become more independent and confident.

Alan, New Routes support worker

Left to right: David, Matthew, Jonathan, Robert and Alan, New Routes: Horticulture and Woodwork Project, Victoria Park, Warrington

A group of six young people are in their fifth year of the Duke of Edinburgh Award, now doing their Gold Award.

It was started here as we found there wasn't anything for young people to do after they left college. In the past people would have stayed at home with their families or gone into long stay institutions. We had this group of young people in their twenties and wanted to find something for them. Now they can do five years of the Duke of Edinburgh Award. They have worked together for five years: gardening, painting at a local residential home for old people, completing all parts of the Award.

Last year they went to Tenerife as their residential section for the Gold Award. They supported some younger children on holiday from Rainbow Trust Children's Charity, a charity that supports children who are terminally ill or have a long-term illness, and their families. They made sure the children were having a good time and helped out where they were needed. In the evenings they made sure everyone was up and dancing. I was worried it would be terribly sad but we all got along so well and laughed so much it was hard to feel sad.

At 25 years old they have to stop the Duke Of Edinburgh Award. They can go on to work at the MacIntyre run café, or our art gallery shop. To be truthful there isn't a lot of opportunity for them to find work.

Lynn, New Routes support worker

—

Adam goes to New Routes three times a week to do his Gold Duke of Edinburgh. He's been coming for four years. His difficulty is with communication. He know's what he wants to say but he struggles to find the words; often he just nods. Now he is so settled into the group that he finds the words more easily and can join in. Jonathan and Adam go off to work together when I arrive. Adam leads the way, he points to the apples that need to be picked up and the two of them work quietly together, without supervision.

Polly

—

Because we're all working, everyone just gets on with the jobs around the garden. They try different tasks, and we don't tell them what to do, we work together. Jonathan is relaxed when he's at New Routes — he bounces around the garden — and he takes that home. He lives with his Mum.

Alan, support worker with New Routes since 2000

Adam, Duke of Edinburgh Award. New Routes: Horticulture and Woodwork Project, Victoria Park, Warrington

Adam and Jonathan

Kenny, New Routes: Horticulture and Woodwork Project, Victoria Park, Warrington

Top: Oliver and Andrea are doing their Duke of Edinburgh Gold Award along with three friends. They help with all work at New Routes: growing plants, clearing, weeding, etc. Oliver says: 'After we finish our Gold Award we're not sure what we'll do, or if we can stay together as a group or not. We went to school together.'

Polly

—

Bottom: David is supported by MacIntyre. He loves animals. About fourteen years ago MacIntyre made a link with Walton Hall and Gardens Children's Zoo, Warrington. Two people go with a member of staff and help to feed the animals and clean out their runs. David needs a lot of encouragement and enthusiasm. He enjoys the conversations with staff at the zoo. Peter, a zoo worker, has built up strong relationships with the people who come to do work experience. Peter speaks clearly to David and leaves messages directly for him at the learning centre.

Joanna, support work, New Routes, Warrington

Oliver and and Andrea, Duke of Edinburgh Gold Award. New Routes: Horticulture and Woodwork Project, Victoria Park, Warrington

Peter and David, Walton Hall and Gardens Children's Zoo, Warrington

Stuart and David, Printing Enterprise, Holmewood Community Centre, Derbyshire

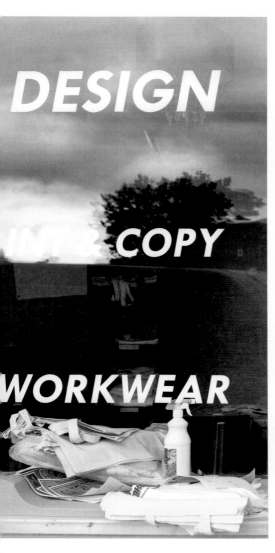

(Left to right) Stuart with Tracy and David

Left to right: Cavan, Carl, Ravinder, Jeffrey and Adam, Holmewood Community Centre, Chesterfield, Derbyshire

Left to right: Marlene, Jeff, Alan, Ravinder, Gary, Stuart. Background: Lynne, Alwyn, Wayne, Philip, Holmewood Community Centre, Chesterfield, Derbyshire

<u>Previous spread:</u> This is our weekly meeting. This week we discussed some current affairs items (halal meat in Subway, a school teacher being killed, and other things. We don't shy away from controversial issues!). We always discuss 'good news/bad news' and plan forthcoming events. Sometimes they get a bit stuck into the current plot of *Coronation Street*, or some other soap, and we have to remind them that we are here to talk about real life events.

Lisa, front-line manager, Holmewood Community Centre, Derbyshire

James lives in his own house next to Lewis. They used to share a house, but James's needs are so complex it didn't work. We tried to arrange the house to suit them both, but it just didn't work. There were many occasions when James and Lewis became upset and frustrated, putting themselves, and staff at great risk of being hurt.

I asked staff to write up every time this happened and we discovered that most were happening because the boys' sensory needs were not being met: they each had very different needs. James is hypo-sensitive, which means under sensitive. He does not have a developed proprioceptive sense, so he doesn't understand that this is the end of his finger, or that that is where the floor is, etc. He therefore doesn't understand his own strength and constantly wants to push to get a sensation. He also cannot cope with picture and noise at the same time because of the way his brain works. We needed to find a permanent solution for the boys, and I found this house with their individual needs in mind. There is not a cure for autism – this is who they are. I am very proud that we look at the person first and the disability after. With my team we do not say, 'He hit me', but we ask, 'Why was he upset?'

James loves to spend time with the staff. He wants to have a hug when I go in. James has happy sounds, which are very high-pitched, while sad sounds are low grunts. We also use intensive interaction, which means using the other person's body language and sounds to communicate.

All the surfaces in the house are plain. James doesn't like things out of place. The furniture has to be break-proof, and the curtains are stuck with Velcro, so they can be pulled off. James loves nothing more than a big plate of fresh broccoli, carrots, olives and avocado.

Supported living offers them both flexibility and their budget is assigned to them as individuals. They choose support staff and how they want to be supported. Everything is tailored to them personally.

James used to have real highs and lows, now he has become more balanced and is able to express his needs. For example, if he wants one of us to leave the room he will shoo us away, then when he is in a happy or funny mood he will press the alarm system and we come running.

Elaine, front-line manager, Supported Living, Oxfordshire

James with Elaine, Supported Living, Adult services, Abingdon, Oxfordshire

Lewis used to share a house with James but, because their needs are very different, they now live next door to each other. Elaine, a front-line manager at MacIntyre, worked for years with their families to get them self-contained accommodation to meet each boy's needs. They moved in at the end of February 2015. Elaine explains:

Lewis probably has a developmental stage of a one or two year old, and he is twenty-four. He has noises to express himself: if he uses a high-pitched noise it means he is getting distressed.

In PECS (Picture Exchange Communications System), you give me a picture of something and I give you that object in return. So we use pictures to give people information. But before they can exchange the picture for an item, you have to teach them what the item is. The boys have learned to use it. Often Lewis would become anxious or upset, especially when supported to go out. Lewis would do things such as drop to the floor, or run out in front of cars because he didn't know what was expected of him. So our first aim was to use PECS. This was very time consuming. For example, for about six weeks we were showing Lewis a picture of fishcakes, saying the word and giving him fishcakes, so he would really make the connection between the card, the word and the object. We've had to do that with everything.

Each day Lewis's PECS folder is organised in advance for him. He is shown that today is Monday, and small cards with drawings of home, car, etc., are lined up. First we will have breakfast, then we will go out in the car, then we will go shopping. This is a task he doesn't like to do, but we want him to be able to do it. Then he can go and feed the ducks – this is the reward task. Then we will come home. For Lewis, seeing a card with a picture of home is very important, because not knowing when he is coming home can make him very anxious.

Lewis now has some speech: when he wants to tell you where to go he says "Percy", and when he thinks I am being too bossy he calls me the "fat controller". We are making progress. Last week he used the word "drink", and he also says "swimming". He now uses his pictures not only to understand his day but to choose his day too: last week he took his pictures when he went out and used them to choose his lunch. Instead of dropping to the floor or biting our hands to get what he wants, he can now say or show us, "I want my laptop", "I need a drink".

Elaine front-line manager, Supported Living, Oxfordshire

Lewis on holiday at Rockley Sands Park, Poole

Lewis with Su, Supported Living, Adult Services, Abingdon, Oxfordshire

I have known Leonard for three years. He is quite independent: he finds his own way around within his own environment. He lives at Daubeney Gate, (a supported living house) with five friends. He can be quite particular. When he has a bath he has to finish all the soap, so now he works with staff to cut each bar of soap into 8 pieces. Each time he has a bath he gets one piece from the drawer and finishes it. Leonard likes art and craft, bowling and cooking. He loves being out in the sun and quite regularly he will leave a session to sit outside and feel the sun on his face. He does not have a diagnosis of autism, as he came through the old system, living in an institution for many years and everyone was given the generic diagnosis of 'learning difficulty'.

Wayne, senior support worker, Great Holm, Milton Keynes

Leonard, Great Holm, Milton Keynes

Martin has lived at Bradbury since its opening in March 2012. He was the first person to enter the service. Bradbury was purpose built and is located right next door to Martin's day service. Martin has recently had his room completely transformed to reflect his personality.

Martin lived at home until 2012. His doctor suggested to his mum that she find somewhere for him to live before she became too elderly and it turned into an emergency. His mum visits every weekend and on Wednesdays she takes him out with the help of her son-in-law. They go to Martin's sister's house for tea, or sometimes they just go for a drive.

Martin loves *Tom & Jerry* and *Laurel & Hardy*. He says, 'yes' and 'no' and tries to answer questions. He can do a perfect impression of Bruce Forsyth.

Janet, head of service, Bradbury house

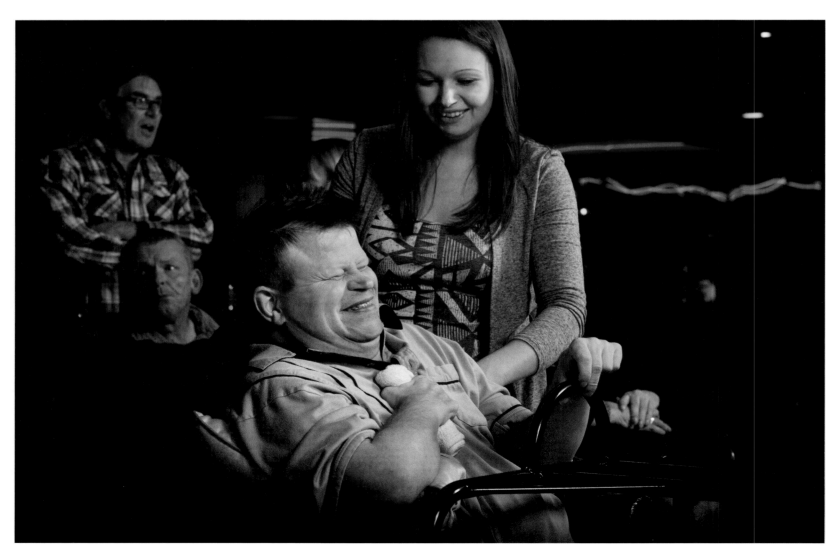

Pauline with Jamie, Endeavour Academy, Oxfordshire

POLLY BRADEN TALKS WITH DAVID CAMPANY

David Campany: Polly, how did this project begin?

Polly Braden: The learning disability charity MacIntyre approached me with the idea of making a long-term photographic study about caring for people with learning disabilities and autism. MacIntyre helps over 1,600 people across the UK. 2016 marks their fiftieth anniversary and so they wanted to work on a project to celebrate that, to look at how social care in England has changed over the past fifty years and to present the challenges we face now.

DC: Fifty years. That's also about how long autism has been accepted as a medical condition.

PB: Yes and now there are over 700,000 people in the UK with autism.

It was a very open brief. I was free to approach it how I wished. It is a complex subject for photography and I wasn't sure if I would be able to contribute anything to the understanding of the issues. So in January 2014 I began with a pilot project. MacIntyre has four schools for autistic children who need extra support. I visited McIntyre Abingdon Partnership College. Students do various subjects in the college and learn life skills such as taking public transport, cooking and shopping at the supermarket with a support worker. As I drove up to the building, a boy called Mikey was lying on the grass in a T-shirt in the freezing rain, while two young men tried to persuade him to put his coat on, or come inside. They were so patient. They just stayed with Mikey, gently coaxing him. A few hours later, just before I left, he came in. His hands were cold and red but he had his coat on and was smiling about something with the two men.

I was nervous to take on this project. I hadn't spent a lot of time with people with learning disabilities and autism. I wasn't sure how I would approach the photography. By the end of the pilot I thought I could make it work. But it's taken a while. Nearly two years, almost full time.

DC: I know your past work, and I can see there are similarities. Much of your photography has been about intimate communication between people, or gestures that you catch between two or three individuals that hint at something without explaining it. This is a book about social care and support in situations that are sometimes difficult psychologically, practically, financially. Does this put extra pressure on your images?

PB: My background is in long-term documentary projects. When I am looking through the lens I'm always watching people's reactions to each other – the gestures, glances, positions, the moments between. I wanted to photograph everyday situations. Playing games, cooking, laying the table. Photographically this can be difficult. When someone is making tea, for example, they generally face away from the camera. You need interesting things to photograph to make interesting images. I had to find ways to observe and show what's going on, ways that would present interactions to the camera without manipulating them. So I found out about MacIntyre's social events, get-togethers, people's work timetables, and all the different aspects of the charity's work. I planned shoots right across the country, at the schools run by MacIntyre, homes, day-care centres, cafés and shops run by individuals with support, sports centres, Christmas parties and even a wedding.

DC: Very often you present two pictures rather than one. Mini sequences. This gives us more, but it also implies that there are things happening that the camera can never get hold of, things that slip between the frames.

PB: Single photographs often present a person as a final statement. The mass media often look for the defining single image of a person but it's not helpful. All of us are in ongoing states of being and becoming. With two images you can at least see the next movement, the next gesture, the ongoing moment, not the definitive moment.

DC: You are photographing people whose interior life might be quite different to their exterior life.

PB: That's very true. There are people who might have difficulty expressing themselves, or who are not concerned with expressing themselves outwardly. Photography has always had a complicated relationship to interior life or mental life, regardless of what we call 'disabilities'. All you can do as a photographer is try to get to know something of the inner life and then hopefully make imagery that is indicative of it, but the photograph itself doesn't prove the inner life or present all its complexity. It can't.

Having said this, there are times when the inner life *can* seem much more available. When I'm with someone who doesn't have much vanity, who carries on with what they are doing regardless of the camera, without being self-conscious, then certain layers of defence are not there. Of course, this is not always the case: many of the people in the book were very aware of my presence and loved to show off, pose, dance for me and my camera.

DC: It's an enormous privilege and responsibility.

PB: It is. Much of what I have been doing for this project has been observing and getting to know people, without even taking pictures. Going back to see them again, keeping notes, listening to them and their support workers. There were many return visits. Sometimes I would be ready to try to make a photograph and people would be having a bad day for medical or mental reasons. I just had to go with it, to enter into the rhythms and the ups and downs of daily life.

DC: We can't immediately tell from your images who is the support worker and who is being supported.

PB: I tried to avoid signaling this. Whoever comes to the book has to decipher things for themselves, which is not unlike the interactions that I am trying to depict – interactions that don't always flow freely or easily between people. The challenges of misunderstanding are there for the viewer/reader too.

DC: That is very different from the photography of mental disability coming from institutions of old, which was so often about fixing, categorising, demonising.

PB: That's the difficult legacy and the challenge. There is no correct way to photograph anybody. One must simply try to understand, and find visual forms that might help others do the same. There is a real emphasis on hands in the book. Hands are indicators not just of interactions but of emotion. Taking the emphasis off faces allows one to see much more of the whole person. Communication can be a physical thing. Expression doesn't come just through the face.

DC: There are hardly any pictures in the book you would call 'portraits', really.

PB: Right. If you are photographing people doing things, the flow is often through the hands from one person to another. MacIntyre has developed particular ways of interacting through hands. For example, if a person is being shown how to use a camera, they should hold the camera themselves, with the support worker's hands placed secondly to guide if necessary. Then the support worker can move back wherever possible to allow independence. You don't do the activity for someone; your hands are there to help, to reassure. So hands can be an indicator of good care and support.

DC: I can see you developed particular ways of lighting.

PB: I tried to find a way to light interiors the way they feel to the people living in them. Through a camera a room can often look overbearing, because the lens takes in every detail equally. I wanted to let backgrounds fall into the background. Some of the photos were carefully planned. For example I would use a dark cloth background so that me, and by extension the viewer, are really free to concentrate on what is going on between the people in the pictures. It's a sort of visual equivalent of intense concentration, that state of mind when what's around you seems to disappear.

But I could only plan to a small extent. For a few days my photographic assistant and I were at Endeavour Academy, a school for autistic children. I couldn't say to the children: 'OK we've set up the studio, now come and have your photo taken over here.' It doesn't work like that. So we would carry the lights and the background and set them up around people, as they were doing their activities. Sometimes they would finish before we were ready. Sometimes it worked wonderfully well.

DC: As in the photographs where Pauline is encouraging Jamie to taste and smell the chocolate bits in the cookie dough.

PB: Jamie is completely absorbed in all the sensations he is feeling. We can't actually feel that through the photographs but we can empathise, and we can see that Pauline is feeling great empathy for Jamie.

DC: How did you approach the writing that accompanies the images?

PB: There are many stories in the writing that are about difficult situations in peoples' lives. I am trying to take photos about support at the best it can be, but not to gloss over the profound problems in the provision of care and support and the challenges around this as well. The project is trying to *look* at what can be achieved for people when they are given good support, and to *talk* about what happens when they are not.

DC: In nearly everyone's extended family there is someone, somewhere, with a learning disability or autism and yet we seem to live in a media culture – everything from movies, to fashion, advertising and television – where it rarely comes up. This itself can be a source of stigmatisation, making the conditions appear to be less common and more specialised than they really are.

PB: Yes, as I mentioned, in the UK there are over 700,000 people with autism and this number seems to be increasing. There are 1.5 million people with a learning disability in the UK. Only 20% of people with a diagnosed learning disability have a job and only 15% of adults with autism are in paid work. Despite this, 65% of people with learning disabilities say they would like to be in work. So there is a long way to go. In the book I photographed a man named Alan leading a workshop. He had been out of work until he turned 40 years old. Then, with a small amount of help, he learned to use the bus independently, to get to and from meetings. Today he plans and presents at workshops, and recently he got married. MacIntyre Catering has six people with learning disabilities helping to prepare lunches for up to 500 people a day. Many of the people I met aspire to work and live full lives. This is achievable with the right support.

The coffee shop opened in 1988. I started working here in 1990. When we first opened there was nothing like this, it was quite unique. Some people would walk in, take a look around and walk straight out again. Or they would talk to me and ignore the two people standing next to me because they had a learning disability. Sometimes people are very condescending, but our guys are very clued up on how to handle it. I have had a person with a disability working in the café who refused to serve another person with a disability because they said they looked too scary. Now people don't see us as a learning disability café. I have seen people finish their lunch and then suddenly clock the people working here while drinking their coffee.

Over a week, 52 people are supported to work in the café. We have a staff team of nine. Some come for a day a week, others for more. They always come for the whole day. In the morning when everyone arrives they check the jobs board. Each person's name is on the board with their tasks for the day. They find the sequencing board for that task. It is a step-by-step guide with pictures and short clear sentences. This allows people to be independent. Some people just stop and stand still if they are stuck, others shout for help. We always keep an eye on everyone. They have their preferred tasks but learn about taking turns and supporting their colleagues.

The café makes a contribution to the MacIntyre charity. The people we support do not earn money – they are funded to come to the café by the local authority. Any money made from tips is used to do fun things together and to buy treats.

Many of the people have been coming to work here for many years. We have an ageing group of people we support and this brings new challenges. People with learning disablilties are living longer and people with Down's Syndrome are at high risk of getting dementia. We try to keep work accessible for as long as possible.

Having the café as part of the neighbourhood has many benefits. One lady came in a few years ago, she had just lost her mother and became the carer for her sister who has Down's Syndrome. She didn't know how to find support. We put her in touch with all the right people and her sister came to work with us at the café. She has worked here ever since and lives with her sister. We have customers who are really thoughtful, one lady knitted two scarves for two people who work here because she knew they came by bus every day. And likewise there is a regular customer who has dementia and our guys look out for him.

Sadie, head of service, Great Holm Coffee Shop, Milton Keynes

Sarah and Zoe, Great Holm Coffee Shop, Milton Keynes

Michael and Louis, Great Holm Coffee Shop, Milton Keynes

Lucie, Milton Keynes Sports Centre

Jay, Milton Keynes Sports Centre

Michael and James are twins. Before arriving at Wingrave in 2011, aged 13, the boys were in the care of their mother.

'It is difficult for parents to leave their children in a place far from home, but James and Michael's mum has fully engaged with our ethos and has seen how the boys have benefited. Their mum, Mich, and stepfather, Paul, visit every other week, alternating between visits to the school and taking the boys home for overnight stays.

Michael enjoys a leisurely day, taking in events and very much seeing the world through his very active eyes. He is much more inward as a young man than James. He enjoys the feeling of security, including having pressure or some form of weight on his head, and wearing tight clothes. Michael always wears a hat and tucks his arms into his clothing. He has a tendency to hoard items he enjoys touching under his top, such as teddy bears. Michael can also find open spaces difficult to cope with, so it is important that when he goes off-site on trips the environment is not too expansive. He enjoys access to the sensory room at school, as the levels of light and sound can be controlled, and it has many soft things to touch and play with.

James likes free movement and dance. But, like his brother Michael, he enjoys light and will often seek out places where light is prominent, such as the hydrotherapy pool, where the sensory lights can look like beams in the dark room. He then loves to flick water and see its reflections on the light, responding by making happy giggly sounds and clapping loudly. James spends a lot of his time looking upward and also manipulates his eyelids to let light in. This is a great sensory pleasure.

One thing that sets these young men apart is how they clearly love and look out for each other. They enjoy being competitive but also show a willingness to ensure the other is OK. They sometimes give each other knowing looks. Often, if Michael is upset James will seek him out and give a reassuring touch or even verbalise in an authoritative way to 'Stop!'

Phill, class teacher, MacIntyre School Wingrave, Buckinghamshire

Michael with Kim

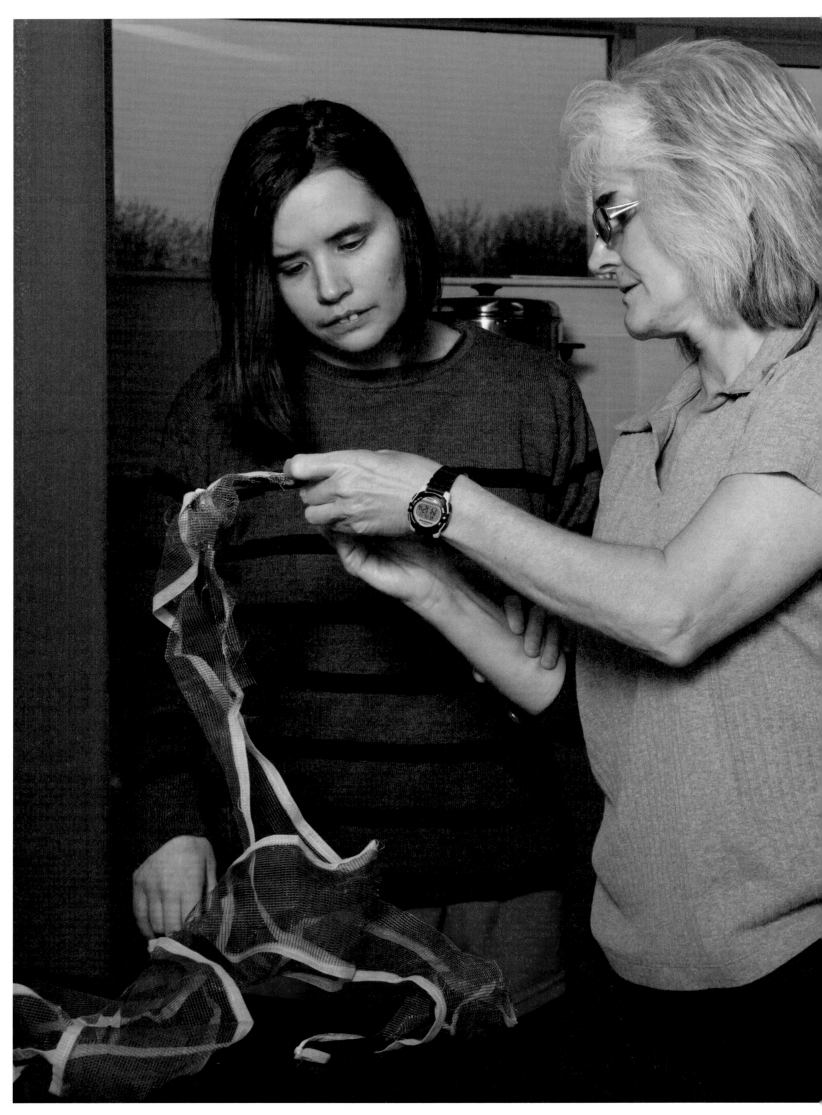

I was born on 30 July 1965. I have one sister called Sally and two brothers, John and Mark, who I don't really get on with, so I don't see them. I lived with my mother until she passed away but remained living in the same house with my auntie Christy, with whom I am very close. She looked after me. My father is still alive.

I moved to Crosby Close, where I now live, in 2007. I have arthritis in one hip and so find it quite difficult to move around. I use a wheelchair when outside. My favourite things are Lego models, both from my imagination and from a kit, and shopping for clothes. I love to wear hats and braces and have many in my collection. I do like company, but sometimes I like to be left alone. I like my own space and will go off to my room when I feel this way. My room is important to me. There are shelves for my Lego and drawing stuff, and wardrobes with plenty of space for my clothes.

Billy

Previous page: Gregory has a learning disablilty. He moved into Anvil Close in 1996. His mother remembers visiting it as a building site. He regularly goes to his parents' house in Battersea, London, and his brothers and sisters come and visit him and take him out. Greg loves to dance – he's a big disco fan. He was born in Jamaica and loves rice and peas.

Hannah, head of service, Anvil Close Care Home, London

Billy, Crosby Close Care Home, St Albans, Hertfordshire 65

<u>Top:</u> Rowland had lived at Anvil Close since it opened in 1997. He was very well known and liked in the local community. He had lots of friends at the local church. He had a sister-in-law in Stoke-on-Trent but no other family. She was too poorly to come to him so we supported him to visit her a couple of years ago.

In April 2014 Rowland went into hospital for a procedure to treat a twisted bowel, but we were told he was unlikely to survive. He did wake up, but died shortly afterwards. We held a memorial service for him at his local church. People from his home and the day care centre he attended all gathered and shared stories, and one of our staff wrote a poem about him. We had lots of his possessions displayed: he was a big Arsenal supporter, so we had his scarf up. He was buried in Stoke-on-Trent, next to his brother.

Hannah, head of service, Anvil Close Care Home, London

—

<u>Bottom:</u> Michael moved to Rowan Close from Homewood in Andover, Hampshire, where he had lived for 30 years. Prior to this he had gone to special schools for the deaf in Basingstoke and Margate. When he had finished school he initially lived at home, and later he went to Homewood for respite. There he lived in a unit for 'challenging behaviour', but as his physical health and condition worsened he was less able to look after himself. Michael has a condition that is like having two horns growing inside the back of your head and splitting the brain.

He moved here on 7 January 2013 and has not looked back. Initially he found it difficult to settle and kept asking to go home, to where he had lived as a child.

Before coming here Michael only went out once a week. He now goes out every day and he loves it. Another difference is that his family now enjoy visiting him and sharing a meal at Rowan Close.

Michael's condition is worsening at a slower pace than first diagnosed, and it is difficult to say whether this is because he is happier and has someone with him always. In addition, having the interaction with staff that he needs, means he has also lost weight, he's more active and he is not being given food simply to keep him quiet.

Sheila, front-line manager, Rowan Close Care Home, Southampton

Rowland, Anvil Close Care Home, Streatham, London

Michael, Rowan Close Care Home, Bursledon, Southampton

Rose describes herself as having a learning disability. She lives alone, independently with her dog in a rented house and does not use day services. She is very proud of this.

I met Rose on a cold night in November, at a Chat and Eat meeting she had organised with support from MacIntyre staff and volunteers. She was busy arranging the food before her friends arrived. As it got closer to 7 p.m., Rose started to pace and get a bit cross. The two women from the NHS whom she had invited did not turn up until 7.15. As they tried to make their excuses, Rose let them know how she felt about this. She had invited the women to the meeting for people with learning disabilities to talk about signage in hospitals. It was a very productive, frank meeting in which hospital staff could hear directly what worked and what did not for this group.

Rose Ralph is a member of the Reps on Board project in Derbyshire. She is one of the longest standing representatives on the High Peak Partnership Board, having been involved for 15 years. Her role is to be the voice and the link between the local Partnership Board and people with a learning disability in her area.

Polly

—

I wanted to set up something in the community for people with a learning disability so they could find out what was happening. It was also a chance to get together and make friends. We have met in lots of different venues over the years, from clinics to pubs and town halls. About 20 people come along and we invite different speakers. Speakers have helped show us how to keep safe and healthy. Our local MP came along once and helped us to organise a trip to the Houses of Parliament for all the reps across Derbyshire. We set up our own Question Time with all the Derbyshire MPs, chaired by one of the reps.

Rose, High Peak Partnership Board representative, Derbyshire

Rose, Chat and Eat, Glossop, Derbyshire

John lives at Daubeney Gate. He has been supported by MacIntyre since 1985 when he started at Wingrave School aged seventeen. He calls his Mum and Dad twice a week, with support: sometimes he just listens. They take him out every other weekend.

He loves the musical *Grease* and plays the soundtrack every day.

Once a week John goes to Morrisons, in Milton Keynes, with one or two support workers. Many locals and Morrisons staff know him well. When we visit a man approaches with his arm held out, John pulls the man's watch to his ear to listen to the ticking. Wayne, one of John's support workers, later tells me the man from Morrisons recently gave John his old watch but John just put it in his drawer. It isn't the watch he likes, but the interaction with people and the ticking of their watches.

The best part about going to Morrisons for John is seeing Anne. The week before we visited was her first week back after two months' sick leave. When John spotted her stacking some shelves he sprinted down the aisle to give her a hug.

Polly

John with Claire

Anne (on the check out) and John, Morrisons, Milton Keynes

Martin (far right), running the Keeping Safe workshop, Chesterfield

Martin teaches his friends about keeping safe and does a role-play for them to discuss what to do if their bag is stolen and who to approach for help. Martin works for the Keeping Safe project, which provides free workshops for people with learning disabilities to help keep them safe. They also help Derbyshire County Council to train staff who wish their establishment (café, shop, etc.) to become an official Safe Place.

Polly

—

Martin started working for the first time in 2007, when he was 40 years old. Previously he attended a day-care centre daily and lived with a family in supported living. Then MacIntyre asked him to work for them to train other people with learning disablilties to become leaders in their community. Martin now works 21 hours a week. He is married and lives with his wife.

Since having Martin involved in Reps on Board we had to change our notes to Easy Read and we needed to make sure Martin's diary was organised. I used to have to help him with his transport, but now he only calls if something goes wrong, for reassurance. When I see him deliver his presentation now I think, 'he is so good!'

Alison, training and development co-ordinator and Martin's boss for Reps on Board, Chesterfield

—

Before I started work, I was picked up every day by bus and taken to the day-care centre. My mum cooked for me at home. I did some gardening at the day-care centre – life was easy. But I wasn't in charge of my life: sometimes people didn't listen to me and I didn't take responsibility for myself. The hardest thing about working is keeping my diary organised. I always have to have it with me. I hate it, but I can't live without it.

Martin, training and development officer, Reps on Board, Chesterfield

Martin and Helen

Residents of Darley Road Cottage: Andrew, Gerard, Graham, Jean, Chris, Sandi and Tony, Christmas Party 2014, Civic Hall, Ellesmere Port, Cheshire

Paul, Christmas Party 2014, Civic Hall, Ellesmere Port, Cheshire

ONE THING YOU NEED TO KNOW ABOUT ME IS...

I Like gardening

I Like singing and singing

sign ing

I'm special

I Like DRAWING!!,
! COMIC BOOK!

I like to watch

Marvel
Movies

To Travel Independently
to Aylesbury College.

I love Super Mario, Daisy, Wario, Rosalina, Yoshi, My cute friend katy king, traffic lights, Mario kart 8, Making ideas for new Mario games along with updated ones for Mario kart 7 and Mario kart 8

Who I love: Michelle R, Russell B, Vikki S, Amy G, Daniel K, Sally D, Robert C, Grace M, Tyler L, Skye B, Poppy W, Mark M, Zak S, Harry C, Jenny B, Alyson H,

I Like
WinX
THE CARTOON

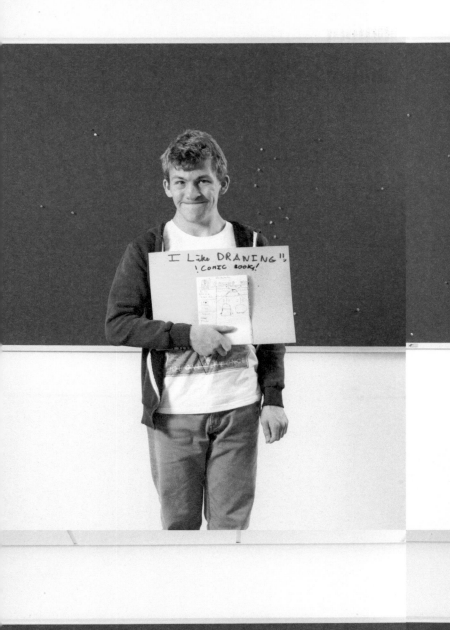

I Like DRANING!! ! COMIC BOOK!

I Like Winx THE CARTOON

I Like singing and sign ing

To Travel Independently to Aylesbury College.

That my lovely family and I sing a Lot to Boyzone / Blue.

I Like to snuggle life to spend time with my family Indeendens

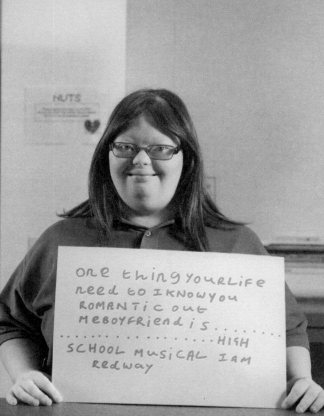

one thing your life need to I know you ROMANTIC out me boyfriend is ....HIGH SCHOOL MUSICAL I AM redway

I'am really good at

gYmnastice

That my lovely Family
and I Sing a lot to Boyzone
Blue.

I LIKe to Snuggl3
Lite to spend tIme
WIth my feniLy
Indeenden6

one thing yourLife
need to I KNOW you
ROMANTI c out
me BOY friend is . . . .
. . . . HIGH
SCHOOL MUSICAL I AM
Redway

I like doing
tapestry
I like listening
to Amy
winehouse on
the wireless
on Heart radio

I work hard

I am kind

DVD DRWHO LB

LOVE TC TO DLEKS

DC MAK

Raymond and Peter, Christmas Party 2014, Civic Hall, Ellesmere Port, Cheshire

Top: Tracey is in her forties. Her mother, who is quite elderly and lives far away now with her brother, comes about once a year. Her dad was her main carer, but he passed away some years ago. As a young child Tracey was put into a long-stay hospital because she had epilepsy and behavioural issues. She moved to a residential home in her early twenties, when the hospital closed down. They could not control her epilepsy and so she was going to hospital most weeks by ambulance. After moving into Crosby Close we managed her medication carefully, and her seizures went down to once a month initially, and now I can't remember the last time she went to hospital with it. She can now stay here for life.

Tracey has non-verbal communication. She'll take your hand to get some paper from the office as she likes to flick paper. If she wants a coffee, she will lean against the kettle to let you know. And she sometimes takes the hand of a gentleman who lives next door, Graham, and walks around with him, but it is on her terms. Sometimes she will push him away or pinch him.

I have known Tracey since she moved in twelve years ago. If we do something different with her we have to introduce it very slowly, otherwise she will have a seizure. The first time we took her to the park it was for ten minutes, the next for twenty. She went to day care for half a day to start with, and she now goes for two days a week. She has one-to-one support: they make sandwiches and do activities that are built around her, so it is very person centred.

A member of staff takes Tracey on holiday every year, usually somewhere in the UK. The staff member will suggest some places, look up things to do on the laptop with Tracey and see when she looks interested. Often we take two members of staff and two people we support. So with Tracey we tend to take her friend Graham. But if we are going by caravan we take two caravans, so they have their own space and can meet when they want to.

Stephanie, lead nurse practitioner, Crosby Close Care Home, Hertfordshire

Taffy with Tracey (right), Crosby Close Care Home, St Albans, Hertfordshire

Amy, Registered Care and Nursing Home, St Albans, Hertfordshire

Kim is a volunteer at Inspired for Training (I4T). This is a MacIntyre training group which is led by trainers who themselves have a learning disablilty. They currently offer two workshops to staff and to people with a learning disablilty: Great Interactions (which teaches people how to interact with someone who has a learning disablilty, how to speak in clear sentences, not to lean over people and to make eye contact, for example) and It's All About Me, Me, Me (helping people to make OnePage Profiles, so that in an emergency or a new situation someone with a learning disablilty can describe themselves in one page).

Kim worked with I4T to help SV2, an organisation that supports victims of sexual violence across Derbyshire. They came to I4T because they were finding more people with learning disabilities were being referred to them and they had no experience in how to work with this group. It emerged that they wanted to ensure their staff members were trained and confident about working with people with a learning disablilty.

We invited SV2 to workshops run by Inspired for Training, Great Interactions and It's All About Me, Me Me. This was good for team building, but more importantly they got to know our group members and socialised together. This left their staff team with additional benefits: Heather taught them some Makaton signs (a language programme using signs and symbols), they learned how everyone has their own unique character and ways of doing things, and we showed them how pictures, photo symbols and signing can help people to express themselves.

Kim who works with us during the workshops explains her role: 'I have a few jobs when we do workshops. I make drinks for people and I am the main person who takes all the photos. I enjoy doing this – I have been shown how to get down low to get the best shots.'

Kim came alive. She explained how to use Makaton, her All About Me pages, she talked about Great Interactions and the kind of body language that would make someone with a learning disability feel comfortable.

Alison, training and development co-ordinator. Reps on Board, Chesterfield

Kim with Helen, Great Interactions workshop, Chesterfield

Left to right: Jack, Holly, Mikey, Joseph and Rachael

Jake with Ian (left), Lifelong Learning, Oxfordshire

When Jake first came to MacIntyre Abingdon Partnership (MAP) College, he needed two-to-one support and trips were extremely difficult. Ian, his current support worker, says: 'Being supported to go out was very difficult for Jake. He found it frustrating not to be able to tell staff what he wanted or how he felt. He would kick or hit out in frustration. Or sometimes he would show how he was feeling by breaking or throwing things. Picture cards helped Jake to express himself. Today things are very different and Jake makes regular trips.'

In Oxford Jake pays for his own bus ticket and leads the way to the Oxfam shop to buy DVDs. He discusses the best routes with Ian and chats most of the way there. On the bus home he wants to sit quietly and look at his DVD. Walking from the bus stop back to the college Jake walks on ahead, chatting to himself. Ian explains that Jake sometimes prefers to be alone, so he hangs back to give him space. Six months previously this outing would have been impossible for Jake.

Polly

Dan with Pamela, No Limits railway project, Aylesbury, Buckinghamshire

I live at home with my Mum, my Nan and sister. I like living with my Mum. I am in my second year at Central Bedfordshire College. A minibus comes to pick me up. Someone from No Limits - a transition service that helps young people from eighteen to twenty-two learn life skills, like travelling on public transport or paying for things at a shop - used to go with me to college until I was able to build up the confidence to go on my own. At college they teach us how to cope in society, like learning how to cross the road safely and how to use the buses. I go to college on Mondays, Tuesdays and Thursdays. On a Monday I do cooking in the morning and some computer work in the afternoon. This week we looked at news reports and had a chat about them. On Wednesdays I work at the *Railway Centre* in Aylesbury. We keep the place tidy. On Friday morning I do some work with No Limits. They take me out and encourage me to do some writing. In the afternoon I go to work at Keech Hospice Care charity shop, in Sundon Park.

Dan

Dan with Pamela, No Limits railway project, Aylesbury, Buckinghamshire

Tina and Moira met in 2005 when Tina ran Pink Ladies, a taxi service for women. Tina picked her up and they hit it off straight away, chatting about ballroom dancing. No one else at the taxi firm would pick up Moira as they said she was too bossy. Soon Moira started going to work at the taxi firm on a Tuesday. She helped with folding leaflets and similar tasks. In 2008 Tina was asked if she would give Moira's elderly mother, Dorothy, respite once a week, and so Moira started going to stay with Tina on a Monday night.

Polly

—

She'd come on Monday afternoon, stay the night and come into work with me on a Tuesday. Moira's mum Dorothy got quite poorly, but still had a lot of physical work looking after Moira. Dorothy was an amazing woman. She was a midwife, and could tell you were pregnant before you had done a test. She was 85 at this point and unwell, and I knew she was worried about what would happen to Moira when she passed away.

Social services said Dorothy couldn't have Moira because she was poorly, so we had a meeting all together with the social worker, who asked: 'Moira, when your Mum dies where do you think you are going to live?' I couldn't believe she asked that with Dorothy sitting there, but now I understand you have to be direct with Moira. I asked her if she thought she would come and live with me and my husband Jeff. Moira said 'Yes'.

I spoke with Jeff that night. He said he'd have her tomorrow. So I told Dorothy that if anything happened to Moira or her, Moira could come and live with us. Dorothy cried. She said none of the family had offered or had room.

Dorothy's health deteriorated. Moira moved in with me in June 2014. My own mum died a week later. That Christmas Moira had a stroke. We were chatting while she was setting the dining table and I heard her drop something, and drop it again. She giggled a little bit, then dropped something else.

The next morning at breakfast Moira's entire face was drooping. She wasn't getting my hand. I called the doctor and explained she has Down's Syndrome and the onset of dementia. Macintyre put me through a course on dementia, which really helped, because when I went to see the specialist, because of the stroke, I understood the scan. A week later Moira had another stroke. When people with Down's Syndrome get dementia it can be very drastic, so it all depends how much attention and work we do with Moira. →

Tina (left) with Moira, Shared Lives, Warrington

→ All Moira wants to do is go on a cruise, just with me, no Jeff. She is very attached to me. This cruise came up, so I spoke to Dorothy and asked if she would like to join us as her health was a bit better. It was hard for her when Moira left, and this would be time together. Dorothy said she needed someone to help her because she can only walk for a bit with a Zimmer frame. I suggested that a friend of mine, who is retired from hospital and who had met Dorothy, could help her around. So the four of us are going away for a month on a cruise.

Tina, Shared Lives carer

Dorothy with Moira

Julia is autistic. She has no known family. She has lived at Oakwood House for the past five years and moved here after about 15 years at her previous service, when it was closed down. The hope is she can remain at Oakwood House for the rest of her life.

She had a very good friend who used to visit her on a regular basis. However this friend died last year. Friendships are encouraged, and we strive to develop these by supporting social inclusion.

Julia is very involved in the local community and is known by hairdressers and other shopkeepers. She has recently become a volunteer at our local dog kennels, where she walks the dogs. On one occasion whilst walking a dog he rolled over and lay on his back, and she bent down and tickled his tummy.

Julia has a very friendly nature and is very likeable. She has certain routines that need to be completed, but also has a mischievous way about her and a good sense of humour. She likes to twirl around on the spot and enjoys flicking light switches on and off, as well as tapping on hard surfaces and touching people's faces.

I supported Julia to buy a new coat last year, and was amazed to find how much she appeared to enjoy trying on various coats. She made a definite choice – she didn't want to take it off.

Julia enjoys being in the company of others and loves just sitting with staff on a one-to-one activity like having her nails painted. She also helps staff in the preparation of drinks for herself and the other people in the house. Occasionally she likes spending quiet time in her bedroom.

Joan, front-line manager, Oakwood House Care Home, Birkenhead

Julia

Julia with Helen, Oakwood House Care Home, Wirral, Birkenhead

Left to right: Mary and Mandy with Richard, Rowan Close Care Home, Bursledon, Hampshire

Previous spread: Richard came to Rowan Close in December 1998 from Tatchbury Mount Hospital, where he had lived for a number of years. The hospital was a home for mentally handicapped people and housed 260 residents. It sat on an isolated five-acre site. Richard lived on a ward with lots of other people, where his basic needs were met. However, his clothes, if he wore any, were dirty, and he usually lived in his pyjamas, although there was no way of knowing if they belonged to him. He had a locker by his bed but no wardrobe. It was noisy, and people rocked in their chairs and shouted all day. He only left the hospital to go on an outing in summer.

At Rowan Close, a purpose built bungalow, Richard has his own room with a wardrobe full of his own clothes, a television and music system and a spacious lounge he shares with five other people. A good day is when he wakes up smiling and clapping. He loves people, music and animated films. Richard enjoys going out and looking in shops. One of his favorite places is the local sea-life centre and most of all, he likes being able to spend time in the sensory garden at Rowan Close with the staff. Although Richard needs full support in everything, he now leads a fun-filled life.

Sheila, front-line manager, Rowan Close Care Home, Hampshire

—

Bottom: Like Richard, Larson came to Rowan Close in December 1998 from Tatchbury Mount Hospital, where he had lived since 1979. At first he was very nervous and quiet, as he had been picked on and hit by other people on the ward at Tatchbury. He is now very relaxed and smiles when you talk to him.

Larson enjoys holding your hand, which is something he would never do when he first arrived. He would jump if he heard a sudden noise.

Larson's parents lived in Zimbabwe until a few years ago. Now they visit him at least once a month during the summer, and in the winter they go abroad but are always contactable.

Some days, when the sun is shining through his window, I see Larson wake up smiling and I know it is going to be a good day for him. He loves to interact with people and enjoys going out in the community. Most of all Larson loves coming home to his own bed at night — he gets upset if he needs to be away from home.

Sheila, front-line manager

Thomas with Alexandra, MacIntyre Abingdon Partnership (MAP) College, Oxfordshire

Sheila with Larson, Rowan Close Care Home, Bursledon, Hampshire

Left to right: Raúl, Farrise and Claire, Endeavour Academy, Oxfordshire

The Lifelong Learning Centre at Ampthill offers a broad curriculum for people in a wide range of vocational, work-based and community settings.

Scott has been working with the warden at a local nature reserve. He helps with the bat boxes, and they've been pond dipping too. When he first came he needed one-to-one support, whereas he can now go in a group of three-to-one. It has taken three years to get him calm enough to be able to do this. He sees his family every three to four months.

Robin, front-line manager. Lifelong Learning Centre, Ampthill, Bedfordshire

Charlie, Lifelong Learning Centre, Ampthill, Bedfordshire

Lesley and Becky

Becky did her Duke of Edinburgh Bronze and Silver Awards. She was too old to do her Gold Award, it's only available to under 25 year olds. Now Becky, Stephanie and Lesley come to day services. Becky works in the MacIntyre Art Gallery in Warrington once a week. All three make clothes on another day. Lesley's embroidery is fabulous, she copies pictures from a book and matches the colours perfectly. All three girls live at home with their families.

Joanna, senior support worker, dance and movement, Warrington

left to right: Becky, Stephanie and Lesley, dance and movement class, St Elphin's community centre

Ken, Alex's support worker until recently, was found specifically for Alex because he was musical. Ken introduced different instruments to Alex and helped him grow musically. From an early age Alex said he would be on stage. On the way here one of his flatmates was helping put the instruments in the car and asked if Alex was going to help. Alex replied, slightly dismayed, 'But I'm the drummer.' On holiday we were watching a band play. Alex was concentrating on the drummer. Suddenly he got up and said, 'he's rubbish' and walked out. He's not big headed, he just wants to work as a drummer, to be on stage and he has total confidence that he'll be spotted one day and I'm sure he will be.'

Andrea, Alex's Mother

—

I started playing the drums when I was nine years old. My Dad found me lessons. I listen to the music then copy the rhythm. I have an electric drum set in the attic at Manchester Road [the house Alex shares with three other autistic boys].

Alex

Alex with Ken

Reps on Board is a training and development project for people with learning disabilities. These people become the 'Reps', who represent others with learning disabilities on local partnership boards.

Polly

—

I myself have a learning disablilty. I am part of the Reps on Board project in Derbyshire. I am also on the North East and Bolsover Local Partnership Board, and one of my jobs is to make sure that other people with a learning disablilty are included in things and kept in touch with what is happening. I used to live in Nottinghamshire, where I was chair of a group called Notts Pioneers, which was organised by Nottingham County Council. I thought it would be great to have a group where people could meet up, and I successfully applied for a Scope Millennium Award. This enabled me to set up Amongst Friends. We had great fun and it helped boost people's confidence. After just over a year I had to move to Derbyshire because of my dad's job, and sadly the group fell apart.

But soon after moving I got involved with the Derbyshire Learning Disability Partnership Board. I just knew I wanted to set up a group here. With help from my family and volunteers I did this, in 2014! We meet every fortnight at the Chesterfield Community Centre. It is close to the bus station so it's easy for people to reach us. The members choose the activities. We have so far had craftwork, games, bingo, bowling, a disco and a Christmas meal together. Our last meeting fell on Bonfire Night, so we just had to go to a local firework display. For the future we have planned cooking sessions, sports and swimming, to learn about welfare benefits and budgeting, have a first aid training session and workshops for keeping safe.

All this has helped us get to know each other and gain confidence. We want the group to be friendly, useful and fun for all. Members are encouraged to voice their opinions and choices at all times. It is their club. One of the great things about the club is that volunteers, support workers and club members all work together. The help I have received for my own difficulties has given me a lot more confidence, self-esteem and fun times, which I hope others will be able to enjoy too.

Alan, Reps on Board

Alan with members of Amongst Friends, Chesterfield fireworks display, Derbyshire

Liam is a cool yet complex young man. He has Asperger's with other mental health conditions mixed in. He had a very difficult time in mainstream education followed by specialist schools, before coming to No Limits in Luton.

When I first met Liam he was quite withdrawn and spent his time sat in a dark room on his computer, eating lots of chocolate and drinking cans of energy drinks. He often displayed inappropriate behaviours and would refuse to engage in any learning.

At the time of referral Liam was getting into serious trouble with the police: he would make hoax calls resulting in armed response units coming out to him. I've worked closely with Liam with regards to coping with community situations – avoiding calling negative attention to himself. He has clearly made huge steps forward and is no longer putting his life in danger.

It took a few weeks to gain Liam's trust and to develop a relationship. I used his likes and his good sense of humour to encourage him to come out into the community. We visited museums such as Imperial War Museum Duxford, where Liam made videos and acted as a video journalist in front of the camera, telling the story of certain planes and giving his opinions. Liam finds schoolwork unnecessary, but he enjoys this kind of activity.

I also taught Liam to swim. After an insecure start in the water, soon he was diving and able to swim 30 lengths of a large pool. He gained a lot of self confidence from this.

Liam has an interest in nature so, with his agreement, I arranged some work experience at the Forest of Marston Vale. He learned the importance of work as well as timekeeping, appropriate behaviours and personal achievement. He started off litter picking and ended up helping to create structures out of living willow.

Mark, community learning facilitator, Bedfordshire

Left to right: Liam with Mark and Blessing, willow weaving at Marston Vale Forest Centre, Bedfordshire

146   Richard, World Autism Day event, Warrington

Before coming to Wingrave, Taiye was in a special school but they could not manage her behaviour. She was strapped into a chair for most of her school day. This was recognised as not meeting Taiye's needs and she came to Wingrave in September 2011.

Although able to communicate verbally, Taiye's speech was poor when she arrived. A lot of the time she used her physical behaviour to communicate her feelings. Participating in chat group sessions led by our speech and language therapist has greatly helped Taiye to develop other communication skills.

Taiye's posture was poor, but with occupational therapy and activities such as swimming and trampolining this has very much improved. She also needed to walk to calm herself, and, when anxious, she could run very fast, would physically challenge others and would, for instance, set off fire alarms.

At the prom Taiye was anxious, as she knew she would be leaving school soon, and having her family there was difficult for her. She needed two staff members to walk with her, to prevent her challenging others, but when her family left she was able to be supported just by me. Some students are not able to handle parents at school (they are in the wrong place, so to speak).

Throughout her time with us Taiye still challenged others on occasion, but we found that having a staff member on either side and just walking (without talking), sometimes for up to three hours, would help calm her. She had an interesting behaviour pattern which I have not come across before, which is being over-attached to the decision makers, namely teachers, senior staff or heads of service. This was because she knew they were the ones who planned activities, and she would negotiate with them. But when they were not around her anxiety increased greatly and she could challenge as a result. At first this was difficult, but it was important to establish boundaries.

Shauneen, teacher, MacIntyre School Wingrave, Buckinghamshire

Taiye at her prom

Taiye opening a present with Shauneen (left) and Julie (right), MacIntyre School Wingrave, Buckinghamshire, for children and young people aged 10–19   149

Ella is an amazing young lady who has the most infectious laugh and loves music – perhaps because her dad has his own band! Ella was able to read text and had a sound knowledge of numbers when she arrived at the school, but she found accessing learning very difficult. Her reliance on the computer to watch video clips of music she liked was a huge barrier to learning. Ella presented with very high levels of anxiety and found change difficult, so she needed rigid structures and routines. Because Ella has an amazing sense of humour it was easy to build a positive relationship with her quickly. Staff had to be confident and consistent to provide Ella with the security and trust she needed. Once this was established, using clear communication, barriers to learning decreased. Going out could be very difficult but she was able to go swimming off-site and out for a snack at MacIntyre's café, The Point, where she made choices and used her counting and money-handling skills to pay for her snack.

When Ella first came to the school, she found group activity difficult. Staff developed strategies such as using a digital timer so that Ella could know how long an activity would last as well as using photos and symbols to provide information to lower anxiety. Additionally, she had her own portable schedule, which helped her focus on the tasks, knowing what would follow.

Ella had learned some negative behaviour patterns, and as staff built up positive relationships with her they were able to provide clear boundaries, which she responded to positively. This resulted in a decrease of negative behaviour, which only presented when she was not well, hadn't slept or something had upset her. She began to respond more to verbal communication from staff and to use her speech more than physical responses. The highlight of the year was Ella being able to attend her prom with her peers and family to celebrate the end of her school career.

Shauneen, teacher, MacIntyre School Wingrave, Buckinghamshire

Ella with her parents at her prom, MacIntyre School Wingrave, Buckinghamshire, for children and young people aged 10–19

Left to right: Pasquale, Nicholas, Paul, Peter, and Tracey serving food at an event. MacIntyre Catering, Milton Keynes

Jason researches and builds towns where disasters have taken place. He has just finished a fairground built of cardboard and matchsticks. It is a replica of a fairground built near Chernobyl which was due to open days before the nuclear reactors exploded. He has made all four attractions; ferris wheel, bumper cars, swing boats, carousel as well as the workers flats. The real fairground was covered in radioactive dust and never used. A few months later Jason set his model on fire.

Paul, senior support worker, Lifelong Learning, Milton Keynes

Previous spread: On an average day we have seven to eight orders of 60–70 lunches for offices in Milton Keynes. We also cater for events. We did the Mayor's Dinner in May, a lunch for 500 at Volkswagen in June, and we'll soon be serving lunch for 500 people over three weekends at an event at the Stantonbury Campus. We don't advertise – it is all word of mouth. We have a staff of four who support six people with learning disabilities every day. Together we cook all the food, and at events we also serve it. We had a standing ovation at the end of the Mayor's Dinner.

Sadie, manager of MacIntyre Catering and Great Holm Coffee Shop

Paul with Jason

Simon with Paul, Lifelong Learning, Milton Keynes

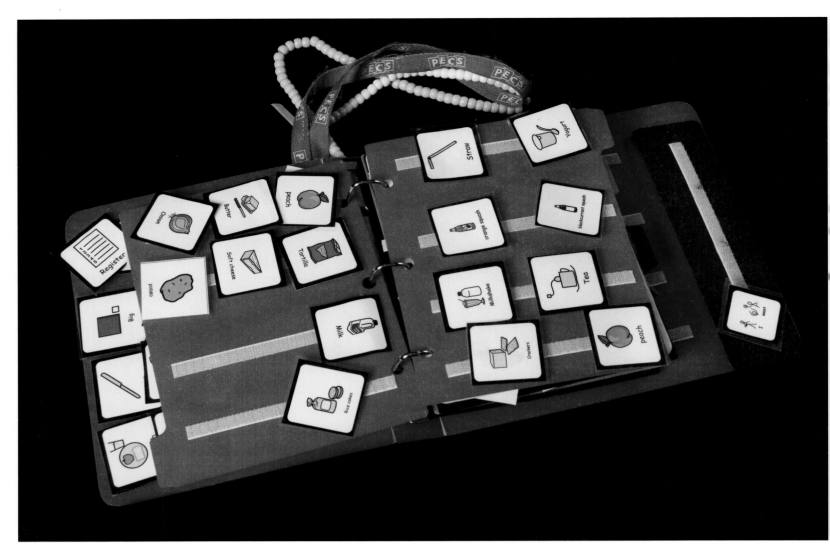

PECS (Picture Exchange Communications System)

Michaela with Adam, Endeavour Academy, Oxfordshire

Jack is the embodiment of the enthusiastic sportsman; he loves anything to do with physical activity and fun. Archery was a great way for him to focus on a singular activity, concentrating on body positioning and sequencing of movement. It provided Jack with the chance to follow rules and safety precautions well, and he even reminds staff when they are not following the rules. Although Jack makes looking like Robin Hood easy, it is anything but. Ensuring that he had the correct body position, and holding that stance whilst taking aim was a huge challenge. We placed balloons on the archery target, and the reward and gratification of a loud bang were massive motivators for him.

Callum, behaviour support specialist, MacIntyre School Wingrave, Buckinghamshire

Chris, Endeavour Academy, Oxfordshire

Mitchell has learned to trampoline over the past year. He now follows hand signals to do forward rolls, twists in the air and seat drops. He closes his eyes when he does a back drop to absorb the sensory experience as he lands on the trampoline. It is the feeling of weightlessness then deep pressure as he sinks into the trampoline which gives him heightened body awareness that he so loves.

Callum, behaviour support specialist, MacIntyre School Wingrave

—

It was very difficult for Mitchell to change his schedule when I first met him. If he needed to wear new socks or if we had run out of Marmite, for example, he would have a meltdown. He uses PECS (Picture Exchange Communication System) for his timetable, but he would stick to it rigidly, finishing one activity after another in quick succession, so we had to build in a pause. We made a 'wait' picture card, Mitchell now holds this happily while he waits.

Recently he has been going to work experience at Horses Helping People. He is faced with new challenges and he is thriving. He loves the interaction with the horses. He gently places his hands on the horse and gives it a deep pressure rub. He leads it round, helps to clean the stable and feed it.

In the past Mitchell had no words, now he says, 'yes' and a few other words. He has started using a computer program called Grid 2 Player. It is very like PECS, but the computer speaks the words. He can use it to answer questions such as, 'What would you like for a snack?' by finding the correct buttons. One button says 'I want', then he can find a picture of 'raisins' or 'rice cake'. He is learning to use this quite independently.

Joanna, class teacher, MacIntyre School Wingrave

Mitchell, MacIntyre School Wingrave, Buckinghamshire

Mitchell (right) with Callum, MacIntyre School Wingrave, Buckinghamshire

My sister Tessa went to live at MacIntyre when she was about six. My parents were terribly torn about it. Having travelled around the country looking for a place for her, they were delighted to find Westoning (an early MacIntyre project) was being set up. Tessa became one of its first residents. There was a settling-in period of two to three months. My parents were advised not to visit or make contact. They had never been apart. I had the task of taking Tessa on day trips. It was the most desperately unhappy thing I've ever had to do: attempting to cajole her, pretending we were all having a happy day out and then having to assure my parents everything was just fine. But Tessa soon settled and home visits were regular.

When Wingrave School was first established Tessa transferred for her school years, and in time went to live at The Haddons, a group of registered care services in Milton Keynes. Tessa's small group of friends all made the same journey. For forty-two years they have been together. That's quite unique and very special, with stability and history that few are privileged to experience. Our parents died at a young age, and sadly our brother at the same time. It was traumatic. Tessa was obviously very sad, but it was as if she had this comfort blanket – her own life, independent of her family. Her routines, work and social life were all in place.

When Tessa and Mark first started to talk about getting married I was hesitant. They shared a flat with James and Keith and all seemed very happy together. I didn't want anything to spoil that. But they are a determined pair, set on 'living their dream'. They knew they wanted church bells, ribbons on the car, balloons, a veil for Tessa and daleks on the wedding cake.

Their wedding day was wonderful: they both just radiated joy. They were the centre of attention, but so relaxed. They made their speeches and performed the most enchanting first dance, with a tangible feeling of love from everybody there – family, staff and friends. Married life is very much the same as it was before: their rooms have been reorganised and revamped, but they continue to share their flat with James and Keith.

Caroline, Tessa's sister

Caroline and Tessa on Tessa's wedding day, Tring, Hertfordshire

I met Mark at Westoning. He used to work at the farm there, with James. He let the chickens out and James had to chase them back in. He helped with the horse riding. We were just friends. At Wingrave I looked after little children and we did horse riding – there was a big school there.

We talked about getting married. Mark asked me first. He still likes his friends. Mark said to me, 'Would you like to be my girlfriend?' We were girlfriend and boyfriend first, before we got married. And then we agreed to get married. He thinks I'm a lovely girl. I said yes. He picked the right one. I think I picked the right one, I wanted him. I'm going to stick with him.

I like it when he's happy. He likes his dancing, going to dancing classes. We love each other. He likes to take me out at weekends to the city centre. He's an untidy person – he throws his junk around. He's kind, he worries too much about his wife, that's why he loves me. When he makes drinks he takes the sugar pot in the lounge and doesn't put it back. He should take the sugar pot back. I don't tell him off. I can't shout at my husband. I don't want to tell him off. I just want to be kind. I say to Mark 'go and make your wife a drink' and he goes into the kitchen and makes one. That's the way to do it. And also he helps me with cooking the Sunday lunch.

Caroline, you made the wedding dress. I remember when I came down for the weekend, I saw how you made it. First we had to try it on, then you made the underneath bit, the petticoat. The top bit was cream. The dress had lace. I had the veil, and we had clips to hold the veil and a headband and flowers. And the shoes were gold. Mark had a top hat, and his best suit, and silvery shoes. Mark's family were there, and my family.

Mark was waiting in the church with the vicar. He was waiting for the bride to come down the aisle, that's when the wedding march played. I liked the church and seeing my husband down the bottom. All our friends were there. Some of the staff were crying – that means they were happy. We said the words correctly. We practised them in my flat before we got married. I liked the bit outside: there were lots of people taking photos of me and Mark. Mark got all excited about the car – there were ribbons on the car. We went to the reception at Great Holm. That's where me and Mark did the first dance. I copied the DVD *Dirty Dancing*. Mark goes to dance classes every Monday. Mark did his speech and I did mine. We went to cut the cake. There was lots left over. We saved some for the flats. All the flats had some. It got shared out. →

Mark, Tring Church, Hertfordshire

→ When we got back to the hotel, there was a surprise — flowers around the bed and balloons. He keeps messing around with it. I kept laughing at Mark — he was trying to throw the flowers around me. I got a bit fed up with it — he got carried away, that's why he's excited. He's happy now he's married.

We love each other. Being married doesn't feel any different. That's it. It makes me feel happy. Mark's already got his name, so his wife will be Tessa Jane Ahrens, that's mine and Mark's choice. I used to be Warhurst — not anymore now. When my bus pass has run out they're going to change my name on it.

I like living at Great Holm, I just like it. Me and Mark, we do all the flat jobs. James doesn't do much. He likes the dishwasher, he doesn't like cleaning the kitchen. Keith helps. Mark's a superstar at cleaning, he calls himself that. He lets me go and do the bathroom so he does the kitchen. In the evening we clean the flat first and then we chill out and do the laundry. I cook on Mondays at the moment. We all eat together but sometimes James goes out. They're not bad. Keith likes coming in my lounge. He likes *Home Alone* and stuff like that — it makes him laugh.

Tessa

Tessa and Mark, Tring Church, Hertfordshire

I AM BECAUSE YOU ARE

Sophie Howarth

There is a Zulu proverb - umuntu ngumuntu ngabantu - that is often translated as 'a person becomes a person because of people', or more poetically as, 'I am, because you are'. It relates to ubuntu - a philosophy which the human rights campaigner and Nobel Laureate Desmond Tutu describes like this:

> It is the essence of being human. It speaks of the fact that my humanity is inextricably bound up in yours. A person with ubuntu is open and available to others, affirming of others, does not feel threatened by others, for he or she has a proper self-assurance that comes from knowing that he or she belongs in a greater whole. They know that they are diminished when others are humiliated, diminished when others are oppressed, diminished when others are treated as if they were less than who they are.

Polly Braden's photographs show ubuntu in action. She offers us a glimpse into a world where people live and work together in ways that affirm and enlarge the humanity of everyone involved. In these photographs we see those who are more able helping those who are less able to master everyday skills, build relationships and enjoy fulfilling lives. We also see those who are more vulnerable helping those who are less vulnerable practice attentiveness, grow in confidence and enjoy a deep sense of purpose.

This book takes its name - Great Interactions - from a phrase the charity Macintyre uses to describe its way of supporting people in its care. 'Great' isn't used to mean epic or extravagant, but to show a commitment to make each and every experience between people, whether opening a door or making a cup of tea, as luminous as it can be. 'Interactions' emphasises the shift away from thinking about actions to be completed - dressing, bathing, hoisting, driving, eating or taking medication - to the quality of human *interac*tions: how we offer encouragement through eye contact, how we hold or guide someone's hand to learn a new skill, how we laugh or let off steam together, ask for or offer a squeeze of solidarity. One support worker described the philosophy of great interactions to me: "It's not what you do, its the way that you do it."

Ensuring great interactions every moment of every day is highly skilled work, honed by practice, feedback and reflection. The support workers we see in these photographs are experts in understanding the complex needs of each person in their care, and helping them establish safe and familiar routines, which slowly and gently enlarge as their confidence and abilities grow. Recent research confirmed that talented support workers are often more introverted than the average person, a finding which tallies with their strong capacity to observe, reflect and self-correct. They don't jump in to do things for someone else, when they could stand beside them supporting them to do it for themselves. Instead they take their lead from the person they are supporting, reassuring and encouraging them to discover their own best capacities. Look at Pauline helping Jamie to cook, Lisa supporting Rebecca to communicate or Ian out shopping with Jake, and you see a set of deeply honed skills at work: reassuring eye contact, deep listening, mindful observation, and respectful positioning.

Most people do support work because of their concern for others, but doing it well involves overriding a natural instinct to fix things for someone else. Standing back can be the hardest part of the job. "It can be difficult to watch someone take ten minutes to butter a slice of bread - but that's what support work is all about, resisting the urge to help, and allowing the person the satisfaction of doing it for themselves," Joanna tells me. She started working as a learning support assistant ten years ago and is now a class teacher at a school for children with severe autism and other learning disabilities run by MacIntyre. Colleagues admire her empathy, energy and creativity: "she is full of new ideas and always committed to making sure they involve everyone". Joanna's face lights up as she tells me about the Enterprise café her students Maeve, Mitchell, Joe, Charles and Harry launched a month ago. "We do it every Thursday now. Maeve bakes, Joseph greets customers and takes orders, Charles prepares the orders and Harry clears the tables. We open the café to three or four of the admin staff at the school and you should see the joy on the students' faces when one of them walks into our classroom and asks for a slice of cake. Initially Charles needed a lot of help using the tongs, now he can work them by himself, hold a tray and remember who has ordered what. I've watched their self-esteem soar as they become more accomplished week by week. I get goose bumps just talking about it."

On the outskirts of Milton Keynes, the Great Holm Coffee Shop is also run by people with learning disabilities. Unlike Joanna's café, this one has been open for twenty-five years, serves up to a hundred members of the public daily and has two pages of reviews averaging five stars on Trip Advisor: "lovely little café", "great Victoria sponge", "very relaxing, friendly staff", "delicious food, good coffee and friendly individual service". It's run by Sadie, who started working there when she was twenty and at forty-five, has no plans to move on. "I've grown up with the people who work here; they were young when I was young and now we're all growing old disgracefully" she says with a grin. "When I first started this job, people with disabilities simply weren't seen in the community, and it felt revolutionary. Customers would sometimes walk in, look a bit shocked and walk straight out again. It wasn't that people were intending to be rude, they were just awkward or embarrassed because they were so unused to being served by someone with a disability. People with learning disabilities had been kept locked up in institutions, sometimes for their whole lives."

Great Holm Coffee Shop has become increasingly popular under Sadie's leadership and now supplies food for a nearby bakery as well as running a local catering service. Success has presented its own challenges though. "Sometimes, when we get a big catering job, I can see that there's a danger the support workers take over all the work and it's not a truly collaborative activity. That defeats the point. The food is important but it's the relationships that matter most. This café exists to allow people with disabilities to make a real contribution to our neighbourhood, and to enjoy the sociability and sense of purpose that brings. The people here swell with pride when they see others enjoying the food they have made and served. Their lives are complex and I need to offer them a great deal of practical and emotional support. But they support me too. I wouldn't be able to do what I do without them. They are a mad bunch and I love them all."

Denise has worked at MacIntyre School Wingrave, for nineteen years. "Doing my job helps me to be the kind of person I want to be," she tells me. "They say the best way to get love is to give it away. That's certainly what I've found. Supporting children and their families has taught me so much about compassion and acceptance and what it means for everyone to have a life that works for them."

"Most children are referred to us because their families are struggling to cope. We offer 52 week residential schooling, with state of the art facilities and one-to-one care 24 hours a day. When parents come to look around our school, part of them knows this would be the best option for their child, but it is still a heartbreaking decision that often brings tremendous guilt. Tea, tears and tissues are a large part of my work."

"My job is simply about seeing each child for who they are and supporting them to enjoy life in their own way and on their own terms. Sometimes a visitor will come to the school and say "What's wrong with that person?" and I look at who they are pointing to and I think, what do you mean "wrong"? That's just John. Every part of him is right as far as I can see."

Denise shares an office with Louise, who has one of the hardest jobs in social care: supporting disabled teenagers leaving formal education. Budgets for adult services are pitiful by comparison to children's services, and many young people end up leaving a residential school to live somewhere with far fewer facilities, creative opportunities or learning support. "The transition out of school is a very anxious time for families. The question of 'what next' is often deeply uncertain, and it can take many years to plan things well. There is so much battling involved, and the families I work with are grateful for every ounce of support and encouragement. At 18 the child's social worker hands their files over to an adult social worker, and too often that person has only met the child once or twice before making crucial decisions about their life. I have got to know the young people for six or seven years by then and I will fight tooth and nail on their behalf. People often have such limited expectations of young people with learning disabilities. My job is to see past the limits imposed by others, and work out what will open up the best possible future for someone."

"I remember a boy called Matthew who was obsessed with food when he was at school. He'd steal, he'd go through bins, he was always in pursuit of something to eat. Rather than try and keep him away from food, I wanted to find him somewhere to live where he could build on his passion. I helped him find a home on a residential farm where he started to grow his own vegetables. It took a lot of persistence to get the local authority to accept this was the best opportunity for Matthew. After he moved there, I visited a few times and saw how much he was thriving. A couple of times we went out for dinner together in the local pub. A couple of years ago he told me he was applying for a college course in catering. And last week his Mum called to say he has just graduated. I feel so proud of him."

It's unlikely that, even with his new qualification, Matthew will be able to take a paying job. The system puts a glass ceiling on the lives of many people with disabilities. If they develop the skills and become sufficiently independent to be able to do paid work, even for a few hours a week, they automatically lose their entire support package. "It's hugely frustrating when you've supported someone so far towards independence only to find you can't encourage them on the final step," one support worker tells me. "I see so many young people leave schools where they have received amazing support, and grown beyond recognition in skills and self-esteem. And then, at 18 or 19, if they are then considered able enough to work, they lose that support. Ten years later, isolation has stripped them of all the skills they developed during their school years."

"We've helped one woman with Down's Syndrome move from fully residential care with 24 hours' support, to living independently in her own flat with just 7 hours of support a week. She works in both our head office and in a local cafe now, and I am quite sure people would be willing to pay her. But if that happened, the small bit of support she has retained and very much needs would disappear, she'd lose her housing benefit, and there is no way she could cope. So she's trapped by a bureaucratic folly."

One of the most touching stories in this book is the relationship between Tina and Moira. The two met in 2005 when Tina ran Pink Ladies, a taxi service for women. She picked Moira up one day and they hit it off straight away, chatting about their shared interest in ballroom dancing. Moira, who has Down's Syndrome, soon started working at Tina's taxi firm once a week, folding leaflets and helping with other office tasks. In 2008, Tina began staying with Moira at home once a week, to give her elderly mother, Dorothy, some respite help. As Dorothy got older, social services expressed concern that she couldn't keep Moira at home much longer, because she was too frail to fully support her. Tina asked Moira if she would like to come and live with her and her husband Jeff. Moira said 'Yes' and moved in with Tina and Jeff in 2014.

Tina and Moira are part of a national scheme known as Shared Lives. Around 12,000 people in the UK take part in the scheme which has been running since the 1970s and matches people who need support with carers who can provide a bespoke service tailored to their individual needs while also integrating them into their family and community lives. Shared Lives carers are paid in a similar way to foster carers in that they are self-employed and are not taxed on their earnings. In many cases, like that of Tina and Moira, the supported person becomes a settled part of the carer's family. In other cases, the carer provides day or occasional respite support. Many of the people supported through the Shared Lives scheme have previously lived in institutions, and often been considered too "challenging" to be part of an ordinary household. Through the programme they finally experience a sense of belonging among family, friends and neighbours. The striking thing about Shared Lives is how everyone feels they benefit. Tina and Jeff say their lives have been transformed by welcoming Moira into their home.

The mutual benefits of the Shared Lives scheme shouldn't surprise us. People need people. It is through our relationships with others that we feel recognised and valued as ourselves.

When we experience the world from someone else's viewpoint, we have the opportunity to become transformed and enlarged. Opening our hearts and sharing our lives with anyone is hard. Doing so with those who have complex day to day care needs is especially so: it requires unusual humility, patience and compassion. But meeting people who draw out our compassionate side is so much more rewarding than meeting people who bring out our competitive side.

The photographs in this book are a cause for great optimism. They are a testimony to the kind of skilled and compassionate support that enables people with learning disabilities to enjoy fulfilling everyday lives. Many of the activities and experiences Polly has documented - working in a cafe, going swimming or getting married - were long denied to those with learning disabilities. The photographs of Taiye attending the Wingrave School Prom or Tessa and Mark's wedding show the joy disabled people both give and gain when they are supported to live life to the full. But most of all this book shows us what it looks like when people really open themselves up to other people, seeing, valuing and nurturing their uniqueness. It reveals the enormity of what we are *all* capable of when we celebrate our interdependence through every great interaction.

Thanks to everyone who supported this book
both in front of and behind the lens.

Polly Braden

First published in the United Kingdom in 2016
in celebration of the 50th anniversary of MacIntyre

Dewi Lewis Publishing
8 Broomfield Road, Heaton Moor
Stockport SK4 4ND, England
www.dewilewis.com

Texts collected and written by Polly Braden
Project Editor: Rashmi Becker
Colour management: Manish Patel
Copy editor: Ariella Yedgar
Photography assistants: Diego Valente and Sun Shi
Design: Duncan Whyte
Print: EBS, Verona, Italy

ISBN: 978-1-907893-86-5